BRINGING UP CHILDREN IN THE CHRISTIAN FAITH

BRINGING UP
CHILDREN
IN THE
CHRISTIAN FAITH

by John H. Westerhoff III

Harper & Row, Publishers, San Francisco
Cambridge, Hagerstown, New York, Philadelphia
London, Mexico City, São Paulo, Singapore, Sydney

Book design: Maria Mazzara

All Scripture texts used in this work are taken from *The New English Bible*, copyright © 1961, 1970 by the delegates of the Oxford University Press and the syndics of the Cambridge University Press. Reprinted by permission.

Library of Congress Catalog Card Number: 79-67034
ISBN 0-86683-627-6 (previously ISBN 0-03-056203-1)
Printed in the United States of America.

CONTENTS

I WAS born in 1933, married in 1955, ordained in 1958. The next year our first daughter was born; a son and another daughter followed. Questions concerning the nurture of our children in the Christian faith have haunted me as long as I can remember. Answers I received to my questions were not always clear, and even when I thought I knew what to do, I found myself doing otherwise. Now, after eight years as a parish priest, eight as an executive responsible for a denomination's educational ministry, and eight as a professor of Christian education, I am still asking questions and searching for answers.

Aware of my inadequacies as husband, parent, and priest, I dedicate this book to my wife, Barnie, who has assumed the larger role in nurturing our children in the Christian faith; to our children, Jill, Jack, and Beth, who have loved me even when I ignored them in my preoccupation with the nurture of other children; and to all parents and children who, like us, live by and in God's grace as they strive to live faithfully with each other.

CHAPTER ONE

THE RADICAL NATURE OF PARENTHOOD

ONCE, I witnessed a baptism in a small church in a Latin American village. The community of faith had gathered; they had recalled God's gracious acts; they had proclaimed the Gospel. And now they were about to make a response. The congregation began the mournful sounds of a funeral hymn as a solemn procession moved down the aisle. A father carried a child's coffin he had made from wood; a mother carried a bucket of water from the family well; a priest carried their sleeping infant wrapped only in a native blanket. As they reached the chancel, the father placed the coffin on the altar, the mother poured the water in the coffin, and the priest covered the wakening baby's skin with embalming oil. The singing softened to a whisper. The priest slowly lowered the infant into the coffin and immersed the child's head in the water. As he did so, he exclaimed, "I kill you in the name of the Father and of the Son and of the Holy Spirit."

"Amen!" shouted the parents and the congregation.

Then quickly lifting the child into the air for all to see, the priest declared, "And I resurrect you that you might love and serve the Lord."

Immediately, the congregation broke into a joyous Easter hymn. But it was not yet over. The priest covered the child with the oils of birth; he dressed the child in

3

a beautiful homemade white robe. Once again the singing quieted as the priest, anointing the child, made the sign of the cross on the child's forehead and said, "I brand you with the sign of Christ so that you and the world will always know who you are and to whom you belong." As the singing continued, the people came forward to share the kiss of peace with the newest member of their family.

What more brave, radical act can parents perform than to bring their child to the church to be baptized? Acknowledging that we are all born to die that we might have life, the parents celebrate in baptism both the child's death and resurrection. Parents know that when they do this they signify their intention to give up their child for adoption into a new family, with a new day of birth and a new family name—Christian. The child will belong now to the family of God.

More radical yet, the parents promise to bring up their children to understand that should their two families (with accompanying beliefs, attitudes, and values) come into conflict with each other, the children are to give precedence to their Christian family. Thereby, parents acknowledge Jesus' warning that the Christian faith and way of life may one day turn children against their fathers or mothers. Furthermore, without the children's knowledge or permission, the parents make their children members of Christ's Church, bearing the brand of Christ on their bodies forever.

When children grow up they may, of course, deny their Christian name and leave the Church, just as persons may leave their biological families and undergo name changes. But just as persons can never change their origins and always carry within them the genes of their conception, so it is that people can never change the fact of their baptism or their inheritance as Christians who have been born again within the Body of Christ.

I sometimes wonder if we would bring our children to the church to be baptized if we fully understood the implications for either them or us. Baptism is more than a momentary rite. It is entrance upon a lifelong journey— a lifelong quest to actualize the implications of a new inheritance. Baptism not only starts us on the way of faith, but it signifies to the whole world that we are among the company of those who are signed, sealed, owned, claimed, and commissioned to do Christ's work in the world. It is no mere individualized experience. We are not simply incorporated into a set of good intentions or new feelings; we are born into the family of God.

Is it any wonder then that the radical act of child baptism is never to be entered into unadvisedly or lightly? To perform this ritual act in the context of the Christian community's liturgical life is to set our children on a pilgrimage of growing up into their baptism, and it is to commit ourselves to accompanying them on that pilgrimage. It is a long and arduous journey we share together with our children, helping them discover who and whose they are and giving them an example of how they are to live.

Not only is it a radical act for parents to baptize their children, but also it is an equally radical act for the Church. The joyful burden and responsibility of baptism is not on the one who is being baptized, but upon the congregation, the baptizers. The Church makes a covenant with God at a baptism. God's gift of baptism will be enacted through the members of the church family.

This should help us understand why we are free to baptize children of Christian parents into the Church, but we are not free to baptize children for whom there is no one to make promises or take responsibility. If baptism is to have meaning, it is essential that we have the presence and participation of believing and caring sponsors, parents, and a community of faith.

But while the community of faith has an obligation to nurture the children it baptizes, parents still do not have the right to abdicate and expect the congregation to nurture their children for them. The only right we have is to ask the Church to help us be more Christian with our children, to help us grow in our faith so that we can live in ways that will help our children come to know who and whose they are.

In the baptismal rite in the *Book of Common Prayer* (1979), following the presentation of a child for baptism, parents promise to be responsible for bringing up their child in the Christian faith and life. They renounce the power of those spiritual forces of wickedness that draw them away from God by placing their trust in the grace and love of Christ and promising to follow and obey him as their Lord. Next they join all the baptized in reaffirming their baptismal covenant as expressed in the Apostles' Creed and by making five dramatic and demanding promises: to continue in the teaching and fellowship of the Church, to persevere in resisting evil, to proclaim the

Gospel by word and example, to serve Christ, and to strive for justice and peace among all people. These are haunting promises. To be reminded of them is a challenge.

Christian parents are called to bring up their children in the Christian faith. The Church has always maintained that religious education begins in the home through the imitation of parents and participation in family and community worship. Other forms of education have been considered at best an extension or supplement to the training children receive from their parents. No matter where you look in our Judeo-Christian heritage it is the parents who have the prime responsibility to bring up their children in the faith. It is an awesome responsibility. Who among us is adequate?

We want to be good parents, but a host of forces work against us. To begin with, we have no choice of which child will be born to us. We have no control over sex, body build, health, intelligence, or temperament. To become a parent is to commit oneself to another human being, sight unseen. Indeed we often beget children whom, under other circumstances, we might not even choose as close friends. Parenthetically, the children have no choice either. Born self-asserting personalities, they are forced to live intimately with and depend completely on adults with whom they might not, under other circumstances, choose to live.

Parenthood is further complicated in our day by the changing roles of men and women in our society. We lack clear parental role models. Further, there is a decline in the centrality of the family; increasingly we share child-rearing with other social institutions. At the same time, the period of dependency on the parents seems to be longer than before.

To add to our discomfort, we live under the accusing finger of a multitude of experts whose insights, shared freely through books, workshops, and lectures, convince us that if we follow a definite plan our children will develop on schedule and that when something goes wrong we are obviously to blame. Every expert has *the* way for us to follow.

To be a parent in the twentieth century is to be anxious and often bewildered. We all want to raise happy, well-adjusted, healthy, mature, faithful children. We long for what we fondly call "the good old days" when there appeared to be accepted ways and a common scheme. Child-rearing seemed to come naturally. Now we have begun to question what it means to be a responsible, faithful parent. If our children's faith must first be the faith of their parents, we ask ourselves, Do we have confidence enough in our own understanding to lead someone else? Two biblical stories have prevented me from falling into despair with regard to this question.

The first is about Jacob and Esau. Recall that Esau was the elder brother and according to custom was destined to inherit his father's position. One day Jacob was bemoaning his fate when God came to him and announced that he would receive his father's inheritance. While Jacob was leaping up and down in joyful excitement, he recalled that Esau, not he, should rightfully have the inheritance. However, before Jacob could raise a question, God had left, and Jacob shouted after him, "O God, God, don't worry. I know you don't understand, but I'll take care of everything. Your faithful son Jacob will help you. You just relax, I'll see that I get the inheritance you promised me." And he did, even though he had to deceive his father and his brother to do so.

Now there are two points of interest related to this biblical narrative. The first, as might be expected, is that Jacob spends the rest of his life suffering from his deceptions. But that's not the point of the story. The point of the story is that in spite of his faithless act, Jacob still gets the inheritance. Nothing can ultimately prevent God's will from being done. For a parent that is good news.

The second story is the Gospel account of the feeding of the five thousand. You are familiar with the story. In this contemporized version, the disciples are busy conducting workshops, while Jesus is lecturing on the hill. As supper time nears, the disciples return to find Jesus still surrounded by the crowds. Observing that there are a number of "fast food" restaurants nearby, they take Jesus aside and suggest that he "take a break" and send the people off to get their suppers. Thus freed, the disciples and Jesus might eat together, relax, and get ready for the evening session. But Jesus startles them by saying, "No, you feed the people."

They respond, "But we're exhausted. We don't have anything left to give."

And Jesus says, "Just give them the little you have and it will be enough."

And sure enough it was!

That biblical story lent meaning to a story told me by a friend and fellow priest. It is a tale about a young married couple who were active members of my friend's parish. The story begins by his recounting how intensely the couple longed for a child and how impossible it seemed that their desire would be granted. Then one day—miracle of miracles—they celebrated the birth of a son. They named the child after their priest, and he presided at the child's baptism. The story continues. One day, the mother was playing with her son on the front lawn near the driveway when their dog broke loose from a chain. While the mother was chasing the dog around the house, the child, unattended, crawled under the family car. The father, late for work and unaware that his son was under the car, drove over his own child. The distraught parents called their priest, and when he arrived he found them sitting huddled together on their bed. He fell to his knees in front of them and for an hour they wept together. After the funeral, he returned for a visit, embarrassed by the fact that he had done so little for them in their time of need. When he arrived, the woman greeted him at the door with these words, "I'm glad you came. We wanted to thank you for all you did for us."

My priest friend explained to me that he began to cry again and mumbled, "But I didn't do anything but sit with you—and cry." And her reply still rings in his and my ears, "But you gave us all that you had and it was enough."

You and I as parents need to believe in that miracle occurring again and again. And it is only because I do believe that I am able to write this book. I would be misleading you if I gave the impression that I have been a model parent or that I have model Christian children. This book is not a success story; neither is it a practical manual which guarantees success. My years as a husband and father are best characterized by a frequent sense of inadequacy. I wish I had had the maturity and faith when my children were young that I have now. I'd like to begin over again. I believe I could be a much better husband and father now, though I'm quite sure I would still be confused at times, still make mistakes. But it is not my option to begin over again. Although I must live with the past, I can only live in the present and for the future. It will do no good to agonize over past errors. I believe I acted faithfully, if not always wisely.

I must continually remind myself that all God asks is that I be faithful. I must also remind myself that to be faithful is not necessarily to be right. For years I worried about being right. I read every book written on child-rearing and Christian education. I followed every piece of advice. When experts believed that stories from the Bible were not appropriate for children, I stopped reading these stories to them. When experts believed that children could not appreciate adult worship, I kept them from attending. Now I believe that children need to hear and learn the stories from the Bible; they need to join their parents at weekly worship and Eucharist.

As a young parent, I accepted the liberal position on child-rearing which told me that my children were not to share my life of faith; they were only to observe it. I thought all that mattered was that *I* pray, worship, study, and perform good deeds. Now it troubles me that while I was doing all those religious acts, I was ignoring my children.

11

I may never live long enough to know what difference all this has made to my children's faith. Based on where I was in my own faith pilgrimage, I acted faithfully. I believed I was doing God's will. That is all any of us can do, and that is all that is expected of us. As we grow in faith and know more, more is expected of us. We must always be open to new insights. What is important is that we make faithful responses today.

This book is not an expert's guide to the right way to bring up children in the Christian faith. Like you, I am a parent. If I have anything in my favor, it is that there are few strains and stresses of parenthood that I have not experienced and many joys and pleasures that I have experienced. And I have been able to read and reflect on what almost every authority on the family has written. This book is a reflective sharing of the struggles involved in being a faithful Christian parent. It provides no sure answers or easy advice; it is rather a testimony to the faith we share in the grace of God—grace needed by us and by our children.

CHAPTER TWO

A JOURNEY TOGETHER IN FAITH

WHAT are we to believe about the nature and status of childhood? How are we to relate to our children? What does this have to do with our children's faith?

In 1900 Ellen Key proclaimed this to be the Century of the Child. In 1979, less than a hundred years later, an International Year of the Child was announced. Even before our proclaimed "child-centered century" has neared its close we are asked to remember children.

For centuries, the state of childhood was unrecognized. Children were simply considered to be miniature adults. Then, during the Age of Enlightenment, in the eighteenth century, children were discovered and placed in a class of their own. Ever since that time, children have been excluded from the world of adults. In our culture we both celebrate and belittle childhood. We project onto it a false state of happiness and freedom from care. At the same time, we feel compelled to help children become serious and responsible. In other words, children are incomplete human beings in need of being shaped into adults.

It is as if when we became aware of children and ceased to treat them as little adults, we also stopped treating them as full human beings. Now they are *only* children. It was a questionable gain.

15

Typically, we explain that children do not know enough and cannot think well enough, feel deeply enough, or act maturely enough to be treated equally with adults. Children, it appears, have little to contribute until they reach adulthood. Then, through the magic of a designated birthday, children become adults. It no longer matters how much they know, how well they reason, how sensitively they feel, or how maturely they act. Because of their age, adults have rights and privileges in the Church and in the world, rights and privileges denied to children.

Moreover, children are considered well adjusted if they are malleable to the adult will and maladjusted if they resist it. For the past half-century, social scientists have engaged in a host of studies on childhood, but the greatest number are in the category of "problems." Behind each study is someone's conviction that if we had done this or that to children or for children, the situation would have been better. It is as if we assumed that the child is only a passive recipient in human interactions.

The discovery of childhood has produced a serious problem; children are not valued for what they *are*, but only for what they can *become*. The less potential a child has, the less value she or he assumes. At best, we pity and patronize those with limited potential.

All too often our concern for children is in terms of the continuation of the race; the growth of healthy, adjusted, productive adults; and the elimination of social problems resulting from the neglect of children. It is not that these concerns are irrelevant or illegitimate; it is just that they result from an unfortunate perception that children are *only* the seed of adults. No matter how humane our actions toward children nor how humane our concern about their healthy growth and development, if our behavior is motivated by a perception founded upon *becoming* rather than *being*, potentially negative and oppressive results remain. An acknowledgement of childhood, then, may result in a denial of a child's full humanity.

Our Jewish ancestors looked upon the advent of a child as a sign of divine favor, greatly to be desired (Genesis 4:1). Children were of value just as they were (Psalms 127:3). Isaiah envisioned the coming of God's Kingdom as being led by a little child (Isaiah 11:6). The psalmist exclaimed that it was out of the mouths of children, babes in arms, that God's mercy was rightly acknowledged and the unjust judged (Psalms 8). Children, in the biblical understanding of God's covenant, were included as equals in God's human family; they were numbered among God's people. God's promise and blessing was their heritage.

However, by Jesus' day, the people had forgotten that aspect of the tradition. Typically, they considered children too small, too inexperienced, too ignorant, too unimportant to belong to the Kingdom of God. Jesus, therefore, affirmed the tradition of his forebears by re-establishing the place of children.

In the Gospel account of Jesus' triumphal entry into Jerusalem, it was the children who recognized him and shouted, "Hosanna to the Son of David" (Matthew 21:15); and when the religious leaders questioned Jesus about their shouting, he answered by quoting the eighth psalm.

Jesus' evaluation of childhood was especially positive. Children were to be understood as ends and not means. "Then he took a child, set him in front of them, and put his arm around him, 'Whoever receives one of these children in my name,' he said, 'receives me'" (Mark 9:36). Jesus used childhood to define the entrance requirement for the kingdom. "I tell you, whoever does not accept the kingdom of God like a child will never enter it" (Mark 10:15), and Jesus also thanked God for revealing to children what was hidden from learned and wise adults (Matthew 11:25).

The biblical witness is not a romantic idealization of childhood. It is, however, an affirmation that children, like adults, are fundamentally children of God. Children cry "Abba" naturally; adults must learn to say it. What unites children and mature childlike adults is that they are both dependent creatures whose life is founded on trust in God (Matthew 19:13-15; Mark 10:13-26; Luke 18:15-17).

St. Paul makes a similar affirmation when he reminds the community at Rome that all believers in Christ are "God's children; and if children then heirs" (Romans 8:17). In the Christian Church a person becomes such a child or is adopted as such a child by baptism into membership and equal status in the family of God.

The biblical tradition affirms that the status of children is equal to that of adults. A person's being, not his or her becoming, is at the heart of the Christian faith. Indeed, childlikeness is the norm for all faithful life.

This issue of the norm is crucial. If the norm for the faithful life is adulthood, then childhood is disregarded. However, if the characteristics of childhood are considered normative, then children are not only of worth in and of themselves, but they also have something to contribute to the faith of mature adults.

This does not mean to imply, of course, that children should not strive toward maturity or endeavor to reach their potential. Each person bears that responsibility. What it does mean is that our status and value before God is not determined by our having achieved these ends. We do not earn God's grace. It is a gift given to children as well as adults. We are made whole and holy by grace alone; throughout our lives we gradually actualize our true condition as persons made new and whole at our baptism. Our position before God is not to be determined by our potential becoming, but only by our *being*. As a matter of fact, Jesus said, "Unless you are born again you cannot see the kingdom." Our problem, according to Jesus, is that we grow up and cease being children. To be born again is to reappropriate the child in us.

To have Christian faith, each of us needs to retain or recapture the imagination and wonder of our childhood. We need to experience again the spontaneity, creativity, and excitement we knew as children. We need to live with a sense of dependent openness; to explore, look, hear, taste, and smell; to experience a sense of awe; to enjoy holy leisure and festivity.

There is so much we have been taught to leave behind when we enter adulthood. Growing up means becoming independent, productive, and rational. To some, growing up also seems to mean repressing their intuitive, emotional, imaginative, responsive nature which expresses itself in symbols, myths, and ritual and is nurtured by the arts. To some, growing up appears to mean living entirely in the intellectual, rational, logical, analytical, objective, active world of ccntrol, prediction, and order, which is nurtured by the sciences. It isn't that our active nature is unimportant. Indeed, it is crucial to purposeful, responsible life. It is just that it is not all-important. Without intuition, emotion, and imagination, we would be devoid of the experience of God and a relationship with God; we would lack Soul. Without intellect, logic, and analysis, we would lack embodiment. Both our intuitive and intellectual natures are essential to human life, and maturity integrates the two. Similarly, dependence and non-productivity combine with independence and productivity as aspects of maturity.

What does all this tell us about passing on our faith to our children? Our children record feelings long before they record facts and rules. They are powerfully affected by non-verbal communications. Long before they understand words they can interpret the tone of our voice, a smile, or a touch to their bodies.

Children live in a world of the senses. They smell flowers and stomp in mud puddles. Children are innately curious and receptive, trustful, spontaneous, and non-productively playful. While destined to be independent, they are not threatened by dependence.

Children do not fret about the past or fear the future unless they are taught to do so. They live in the joy of the present. Children live in the world of dreams and visions; they take chances and create. Until we teach them otherwise, they believe they can paint, dance, act, sing, and significantly, they enjoy doing so. Children openly expose their emotions and learn from experience. They find miracles believable and desirable. They can sense the presence of God, for they live in the world of gifts as well as achievements. They can imagine the Kingdom of God, for they live in seen and unseen worlds.

Jesus asks us to take a risk and blindly follow him, to observe and to copy. This stance is first and foremost that of children. When we argue that children do not know enough to receive the Sacrament of Holy Communion, we seem to forget that perhaps children are the only ones who can fully understand its significance.

Now, none of this is intended to give the impression that childhood is without pain, hurt, or suffering. Nor is it intended to present the world of childhood as a land of fantasy. But what I want to defend is that children possess naturally the essential elements for having faith. The Kingdom of God is first perceived in the world children know best. Children, therefore, have as much to offer adults as adults have to offer children—perhaps more. As parents, we are not responsible to give our children faith; faith is a gift from God given to both us and our children. We are called to live faithfully in childlike ways with our children so that we both might know the gift of faith and live in its grace.

Faith is best understood as perception. Perception is the key to life itself. Through our perceptions we build up our knowledge of the world. Experience is crucial to our understanding of the world, but our perceptions determine what we experience. If we do not believe in God, it is because any experience that might be interpreted to indicate the presence of God is either filtered out or labeled to point to something else. Faith is like falling in love; it is a disposition of the heart that determines what we see in another.

The Church's faith affirmations begin with the Latin word *credo* not *opinio*; *opinio* means to believe, to have an opinion, but *credo* is to set our hearts upon, to hold dear, to pledge allegiance to. The gift of faith is a way of seeing and hearing, a way of perceiving.

Similarly, revelation is not a collection of concepts, ideas, or theological formulations about the nature of God. Revelation points to our relationship with God, to our experiences of God. Dependent upon faith, revelation is God's self-disclosure to us. If the veil that hides God from our awareness is to be lifted, we need to enter a love relationship with God. Imagine a man or woman on the verge of ending their relationship saying, "You do not know me. You never treated me as a person. You never asked me what I think. You never listened to me. You never shared decisions with me." When people love each other, they reveal themselves to each other fully and do not hide behind verbal, intellectual masks.

Similarly, our vocation in life is not to have a particular job. Rather it is to live the life of the lover, dreamer, and visionary who sees miracles on mountain tops and in slums; to live day by day in the conscious awareness of the merciful judgement and inspiration of God; to be aware of God's active presence in our lives and history; to strive to discern God's will and to act with God as a sign and witness to the coming of God's Kingdom. We are all called, children and adults together, to join God in enhancing and enlivening each other's faith, to help seek out experiences through which divine revelation may be made known to us, and to aid each other in the realization of our vocation.

In other words, we do not train our children for a vocation; we do not teach our children God's revelation; we do not give our children faith.

Our sense of vocation, our awareness of God's revelation can be dulled or lost as we grow older. Indeed, the problem does not lie so much with our children as with ourselves. We adults need to be born again. We adults need to be converted to new ways of perceiving. We adults need to be encouraged to open ourselves to radically new experiences of God. And our children can help us!

Some facets of faith are similar to creativity. We do not, for instance, teach people to be creative. Creativity is God's gift to all children at birth. We can lose it, however, and we often need to reappropriate our original gift. I painfully remember a Sunday many years ago when our daughter returned from church school. She said, "Daddy, draw me a table." Tired and insensitive to her needs, I responded, "Jill, you know how to draw tables; you draw one."

She burst into tears. Confronted by her cry for help, I said, "Tell me what happened at church today."

She explained that an adult at church school had taught her the right way to draw a table and that she couldn't do it.

I said, "Jill, blindfold me," and I blindfolded her also. We then crawled into the dining room and began to play imaginatively with the table. We kissed, hugged, smelled, listened to, and experienced that table. Then, I said, "What color does the table make you feel? Make your table that color. Draw what you remember most and draw it big. Now put in anything else you remember." She did, and with a clap of applause and a cheer, I exclaimed, "Jill, that is a real table, and it is your table."

Each of us has to draw our own table. We can enjoy and learn from each other's drawings, but it is very important to be able to draw our own personal table so we have something to share with others.

It is so easy to lose the gift of creativity and so difficult to get it back. But get it back we must. Our sense of God is so easy to lose, especially in our kind of adult, scientific, technological, affluent world, but get it back we must.

We cannot date when faith begins in human life. Neither can we teach another person faith. It is a gift that we share with each other. The faith of an adult may be different in its expression from that of a child, but it is the same faith. That is why, in *Will Our Children Have Faith?*, I suggest that faith grows like a tree, by adding rings. Comparing faith development to tree development seems to fit, because a one-year-old tree is truly and completely a tree. As it develops, it doesn't become more truly a tree; it only becomes more complex. In the same way, one stage of faith is not better or more truly faith than another.

To continue the analogy, a tree's growth depends on its environment. It needs water, sun, and the right sort of healthy soil. Faith is like that; it doesn't develop in a vacuum, but in response to our experiences in the world. Further, a tree grows in a slow, orderly manner, building on its previous growth. It doesn't skip rings or lose rings. Each ring depends on the ones before and after it for wholeness. Fully mature faith has not lost the character and nature faith has at its very beginning; it is not greater faith but only expanded faith.

Now, of course, all of this is only a generalization. Living, growing people are too unique and complex to be put into neat categories. But what may be helpful is the awareness that you cannot tell what stage a person's faith is by how old he or she is. While people do mature in faith, they can also fail to mature. Further, some may develop into ever-expanding and mature expressions of faith, but if they leave behind the characteristics and needs of earlier stages of faith, they will need to return to and reappropriate these earlier expressions in order to remain whole and healthy.

Our lives as people of faith can best be understood as a pilgrimage that moves slowly and gradually through ever-expanding expressions. The beginning, typical of children through the high-school years, I have characterized as *affiliative faith*. In the beginning of our pilgrimage, the gift of faith comes to us when we observe and copy others, when we explore and test; it comes through feelings or sensory experiences in the form of interactions with others and our world. The foundations of faith are found in experiences in which we learn to trust other people, ourselves, and our world, not because we are told we are of worth and the world is trustworthy, but because we experience it as such. The importance of direct experience in the infant's life becomes obvious. Our actions with our children influence their perceptions and hence their faith much more than the words we speak. Our actions frame what our children will experience. While we do not give our children faith, we do influence the character of the faith by how we behave with them.

From the start, a child's life includes others outside the immediate family. Thus the gift of faith is directly related to a family's participation in a community's rituals, symbols, and myths. Affiliative faith looks to the community and its tradition as its source for authority. We depend on significant others for the stories that explain our lives and how our people live. Belonging to a community is very important in order to fulfill our need to be wanted and accepted. In the beginning, our lives are focused on feelings, religious experiences, and a set of beliefs that claim ultimate truths.

As we journey together, affiliative faith becomes *searching faith*. Searching faith, possible for many adolescents, begins during high-school years and extends through early adulthood. It is characterized by questioning, critical judgement, and experimentation. It comes in the form of doubt and the struggle to frame philosophical formulations. Through a personal search for truth, we move from dependence on others' understandings to autonomy and independence. To find a faith of our own, we need to doubt, question, and test what has been handed down to us. We need to criticize the tradition with which we were brought up and question our own feelings and experiences. During this period, it is not faith that is lost, but the expressions of faith which belonged to others and which need to become our own if they are to influence our lives.

As the journey continues, searching faith becomes *mature faith* which integrates the seeming contradiction of affiliative and searching faith. Possible for adults who have passed through the earlier stages, mature faith begins in middle adulthood and develops until death. In this final stage we are governed by neither the authority of the community nor our own intellectual authority, but by personal union with God through free acts of the will. Interdependence integrates the dependence of affiliative faith and the independence of searching faith. Belonging is still important, but people with mature faith are secure enough in their convictions to challenge the community when conscience dictates. However, there is no longer the need to be always critical or negative. Doubt, of course, never ends, but people with mature faith have a clear sense of their identity, and are secure enough to be open both to others and to experiences that aid them in a process of continuing growth and development into greater awareness of God, ever closer relationships to God, and more consistent actions with God in the world. The intuitive mode of affiliative faith is now integrated with the intellectual mode of searching faith.

We all grow by being with others, who affirm where we are and share with us lives of more expanded faith. So it is that we adults need to be concerned first of all about our own growth, and we need always to remember that even mature faith has at its core a childlike faith.

The norm for human life should not be the physically attractive and capable adult, not the mentally bright, rational adult, not the emotionally stable adult. We would understand human life better if the norm were the exceptional physically, emotionally, mentally retarded child. When we begin our understanding of human life with the fully functioning adult we strive to manipulate the "normal" child to be like us, and we depreciate and patronize the "abnormal" child because he or she can never be like us. We need to affirm that we are all exceptional children and that they represent what it means to be human. In that important sense true maturity is being what we are to the fullest. If we have been blessed with other physical, emotional, mental, or behavioral gifts, then more will be expected of us, but we will not be of any greater value. Indeed, only as we remember, recapture, and live out the exceptional child in ourselves will we be fully human.

Faith is God's gift through the community of faith given fully and freely to every child; we have made it an achievement of adulthood. Of course, as we grow older we need, if we are able, to make sense out of our experiences and perform responsible moral actions, but childlike faith will always be prior, for without it neither our relationships to God nor our moral actions with God are possible. Childlikeness is essential for mature adults who would live by faith. The call to parenthood is the call to share the life of faith with our children that we might both receive the benefits of this divine gift.

The Christian tradition neither romanticizes childhood nor idealizes adulthood. But it does assert the uniqueness and equality of both before God and in relationship to each other. In 1957, for the CBC television series "Look Up and Live," Clair Roskam wrote the play *Plenty of Rein*. At its close, the narrator explains, "Sometimes it has to be said 'This child is an individual soul, the co-equal of mine.' Just as all adults bear alone the responsibility for their life and choice before God, so is the child born with that privilege and that burden."

Of course, creatures born of human beings do not become human in isolation from other human beings. It is, therefore, the responsibility of adults to be *with* and do things *with* children, but not to do things *to* them or *for* them. Like adults, children are human beings on a pilgrimage of faith. Like adults, children need others to accompany them on this journey. Children need adults and adults need children. We all need opportunities to act and react with others in a community of love and respect. What the Church needs to model is a way of life that demonstrates that children, like adults, have equal rights before God and all humanity.

The Church needs to evolve a way of life and organization that can witness to the *being* of all persons. A child at any age is wholly human and wholly God's. Not only does that affirmation support the significance of child baptism, it also supports the participation of the baptized child in the Eucharist. Children must have an equal place in the worship and the common life of the Church. Learning and growth need to be seen as lifelong aspects of Church life and not as a phenomenon limited to childhood. Children need to be integrated not only in the sacramental life of the community, but also in the ministry of the Church in the world. Indeed, we need to advocate the place of children in the Church and seek to learn from them. Our question ought never be, How can we make our children into Christians? Rather, it must be, How can we *be* Christian with our children?

CHAPTER THREE

LIFE
WITH OUR
CHILDREN

WHAT is it to be Christian together? What does it mean to share the journey of faith with our children? These questions may be difficult to answer, but they at least are the right questions. St. Paul is fond of describing the Christian life as "walking" (Romans 8:4; Hebrews 10:19-20). In Acts, the Christian life is described as the "way" (Acts 9:2). Christian parents are called to "walk" in the "way" *with* their children. We might all hope that someone else could do it for us, but it is simply impossible to pass on to others the responsibility we accepted at our child's baptism.

A host of books have been written on the Christian family. Most assume that a Christian family is structured in a particular manner and that within this framework men and women must play particular roles. Such writers are also sure the family of today is disintegrating because the structure is changing. I would like to say categorically that the Christian family has nothing to do with organization or roles; it has to do with a quality of life together, a quality of life that can take many shapes and in which persons can play various roles.

From a historical perspective, the family is always changing. Knowing this, we gain nothing by constructing in our imaginations the "perfect family" or the Christian family in terms of outward characteristics. What people call the normal family—a mother, father, and their children, living in a single household; the father, as head of the family, working outside the home; the mother working within the home with particular responsibility for child-rearing—is neither typical in all societies nor necessarily best.

There are many possible healthy styles of Christian family relationships, just as there are many possible healthy styles of Christian parenting. Family and child-rearing practices have been different at various times in history. Who comprises a family, how that social unit is structured, and the roles each member plays are as multiple as our imaginations. How long children should live with their parents, how much attention fathers should pay to infants, what work outside the home mothers should perform, who should be responsible for whose children, and how important the role of the spouse is in comparison to the role of the parent are all questions that have had varied healthy answers.

The point is, we ought not to ask what a Christian family is as if it could be described in terms of organizational patterns and roles. Consider the various types of family setups familiar to us: one parent, two parents living together or separated, and one or two parents with other relatives and/or friends with one or more children. Consider the various self-chosen roles people might play in a family: father raising children, mother working outside the home; one parent playing the role of father and mother; relatives caring for the children and parent(s) working outside the home. Given these diverse family types, our question should be, How are we to live together as believers in Jesus Christ and members of his Church?

What does remain constant in all families across cultures and history is their functions, one of the most important being the socialization or nurture of children. That is what living together means. Of course, that is more complex than it sounds. In our society, we share this responsibility with the schools, the community, peers, neighbors, the church, the government, and the mass media. Even within the family unit, relationships are complex. Children are influenced by parents, parents by parents, parents by children, siblings by siblings, and so forth. Further, what is taught is not always what is learned, and what is taught is not always what is desired. There are always unintentional consequences, and often these are more significant than those intended. No person determines the life of another. Each of us influences, and is influenced. Transformations in thought, feeling, or action occur: some of them are gradual; some are sudden.

Neither are we determined by our genes. The nature-nurture debate is meaningless. Both inheritance and culture are factors in shaping us. Children are as responsible for their own lives as are parents for theirs. When everything is said and done, the socialization of children in the family is a mystery.

As parents we ought not, and cannot, take either the credit or the blame for our children. We are but one influence in their lives, and even that influence is dulled by what they bring to the interaction. Our children influence and control us at the same time as we are influencing and controlling them. They bring their own unique bio-

33

social condition to everything we do and say, and as a result of that interaction, we are all affected in ways that cannot be determined beforehand or fully understood afterward.

Still, through parent-child relationships, we awaken, strengthen, enhance, and enliven each other's faith. We cannot live for our children; we can only share life and our lives with them. And there is no one best way to share life together. Therefore, just as this book will not attempt to describe a Christian family, it will not attempt to provide parents with a handbook on Christian nurture. The home is not a school; parents are not teachers; children are not students. What parents do with their children is not instruction. The home is the home, the family the family. Each home is different. Some families have many children, some none. Some families have many adults living together, and some only one. Some families eat every meal together, and some are fortunate if they have a few meals together each week. In some families, the adults are home at bedtime; in other families they are not. Some families have two homes and go to one of them for weekends and vacations; others take no vacations at all, and weekends are spent working like every other day. Some families participate in the same congregation's life, and other families are split between two or more religious communities. We each may prefer one sort of family to another, but it would be a mistake to say one is more a family than another.

I remember, as a student, arguing with an internationally known social scientist who said that the typical black family was incomplete and sick because there was no father living in the home, only the occasional weekend male visitor. I argued that he had just described the upperclass families of executive fathers I knew best, and I wanted to know why he had implied that these families were complete and healthy.

Economics, historical circumstance, our personal lifestyles, our chosen priorities and commitments, society's demands, and many other factors both influence, and to some extent determine, the nature of our family life. What is natural for one family—a dinner table discussion or bedtime story, for example—is simply an impossibility for another. Children being parented equally by both a mother and a father is an ideal situation for one family and just not reasonable for another. A children's playroom with various play and art activities, and parents with the leisure to play with their children, is possible for some and only a frustrating, depressing suggestion to another. Groups of adults and children of various ages forming extended family clusters for weekly Christian education are an exciting, relevant idea for some and a very unhelpful suggestion for others. Similarly, an intergenerational church school and family worship program with competent, enthusiastic leadership to aid children and parents to learn and grow, to pray and worship together is a reality for some and only a pipe dream for others. Others have written excellent books explaining and recommending various ways to engage in being Christian with our children. I am not attempting to do so. Instead I am only offering a few guidelines that readers may apply in various ways to their own human condition, for their own unique lives with their children.

I have five guidelines for sharing our faith with our children from birth through childhood:

We need to tell and retell the biblical story—the stories of the faith—together.

We need to celebrate our faith and our lives.

We need to pray together.

We need to listen and talk to each other.

We need to perform faithful acts of service and witness together.

Let's take a look at each, but remember, my intent is not to tell anyone what to do or how to do it. Each of us must find individual answers. My attempt will be to help us as adults to understand a few guidelines for shared Christian life and for finding our own ways to be faithful.

TELLING THE STORY

The Bible is a storybook. Basically, it is a love story between God and humanity; it is a story of a covenant made, broken, and renewed, again and again. God as creator, redeemer, and sustainer loves each and every creature, individually and as members of the whole human community. In return, we are expected to love God and each other.

The Bible is a book of faith; that is, the Bible presents a way to perceive life in general and our lives in particular. The Bible is a book of revelation; that is, the Bible unveils those intimate relationships with God experienced by others so that we might share in them. The

Bible is a book of vocation; that is, the Bible gives us a vision of how we ought to live our lives with God and each other day by day.

We need to enlarge our grasp of this love story—to learn it more completely, to understand it more deeply, to possess it more personally, and to live it more fully. This is a lifelong task. But the place to begin is always the same: We need to learn to tell the story as our story. And the purpose of our learning to do so is always the same: to transform individual and social life so that God's will might be done and God's kingdom might come.

As a storybook, the Bible is made up of various kinds of stories. They are myths, apologies, narratives, and parables, to name four. Each serves a different and unique function.

The function of myth is to establish our world. Myths explain that this is the way life really is in spite of any evidence to the contrary. Myths are not false stories. In fact, as the Pawnee Indians were wise to point out, false stories are history; true stories are myths because they are about God. The stories of creation, Adam and Eve, Jonah, and Jesus' birth and resurrection are myths. They explain the meaning and purpose of life. They are true stories, in the most important sense of those words, for they explain our world. Everyone lives by some collection of myths. No one lives with meaning or purpose without them.

Apologetic stories defend our myths. They are primarily biographical, for what better defense is there for a particular way of envisioning life than the lives of those who believe it and live by it? It is difficult to argue with the person who is willing to suffer and die for a particular way of understanding life and its meaning. That is why the stories of the saints, the ancient and modern heroes of the faith, are also important to know and share.

Narrative stories explore the world which our myths establish and which the biographies of believers defend. For example, our myth may tell us that God is a merciful and loving God, but our experience may indicate otherwise. Narratives explore these contradictions and in the end reaffirm the myth. The story of Job is a perfect example.

And last, there are parabolic stories whose function is to subvert our world and the way our culture sees life so that we might perceive the world in ways consistent with our myths. For example, the second half of the Jonah story and Jesus' story of the vineyard have a similar message: God does not give us what we deserve, but what we need. That is consistent with the Judeo-Christian myth of a gracious and merciful God, but it is subversive to those of us who live in a reward-and-punishment world that defines justice as getting what you deserve and has difficulty supporting welfare for fear people will get something they do not deserve.

Of course, there are other sorts of material in the Bible, such as prophetic judgements on persons and communities who live lives that violate the implications of the community's myths. There are songs and prayers that celebrate life as it is lived within the context of our myths, and there are words of wisdom gleaned from experience that support the community's myth. But at the heart of it all is a love story, the Christian myth which must be known, owned, and lived if we are to be Christian.

Our greatest human need and most difficult achievement is to find meaning in our lives. An understanding
of the meaning of life is not suddenly acquired at a particular age. At every point in our lives, we seek and need
to discover some meaning. The whole process begins at
childhood when we learn through stories. For a story to
hold our attention, it must entertain and arouse our
curiosity, but to enrich our lives it must stimulate our
imaginations and provide us with ever new and deeper
meanings. Stories emerge from and speak to our responsive, intuitive consciousness. That is why it is meaningless
to take our sacred stories, or our symbolic narratives,
literally; it is equally meaningless to try intellectually to
discover their meaning by searching for what can be
rationally verified in them. Sacred stories speak to our
deepest, unconscious longings and questions, our problems
and predicaments, our inner and outer struggles in human
life. They exist in the form of truth that only intuition
and imagination can provide, truth just as significant and
real as that which comes through logical analysis and
scientific probing.

The biblical story is a symbolic narrative. That is why
it enlightens us about ourselves and fosters our growth.
It offers meaning on varying levels and enriches our
lives in countless ways. The meanings of each story will
change at different times in our lives; insights will vary,
depending on a person's needs and experiences at the
moment. That is why it is a mistake to explain a story or
tack on a moral at its close. When we use the Bible to
indoctrinate people, we destroy the story and do injustice
to the Scriptures. When we simply tell stories without

39

explanations, people want to hear the stories over and over again. And when we have derived all we can from a story, we will temporarily set it aside until it becomes relevant once again.

What is important for us to remember is that children and adults need to hear stories. It is human nature to order our lives in accordance with a story. Anyone familiar with Chaucer's *Canterbury Tales* will remember that the pilgrims told stories as they went along. Stories make sense out of the chaos of life on the level of the unconscious; that is, poetic stories provide our imaginations with the means for ordering our experiences. They leave us open to new insights and inspirations. Stories preserve the memory of past events and the experiences of the race in a way that allows those events and experiences to help shape our lives.

Stories are basically oral in nature. They are meant to be told, dramatized, sung, danced, and expressed through the visual arts. They are not intended to be read only. We forget that the biblical story was written down for only three reasons: the community was worried that its storytellers would forget the story, distort the story, or neglect some important aspects of it. We need to return to telling stories. We need to become better storytellers so that our children will learn the stories and learn to tell them to their children someday.

CELEBRATING OUR FAITH AND OUR LIVES

Stories are of central importance in human life, and they are enacted through our rituals. We humans cannot live without ritual; our religious life is expressed collectively through symbolic narratives (sacred stories) and symbolic actions (rituals and ceremonies). Perhaps no aspect of life is more important than our ceremonial life. We humans are made for ritual and our rituals make us. No community exists without a shared story and shared repetitive symbolic actions. Our understandings and ways are invariably objectified in ceremonial observances. Faith and ritual, then, cannot be separated. That explains why, when the prophets sensed that the people had forsaken their faith, they attacked the rituals as empty substitutes. But when the people had lost their faith, the prophets called them to return to their rituals. Without rituals, we lack a means for building and establishing purposeful identity; we are devoid of any significant way to sustain and transmit our understandings and ways. Rituals, like stories, emerge from and speak to our intuitive, emotional consciousness. That explains why dance, drama, music, and visual arts are the basic means by which our rituals are enacted. And that is why poetry more than prose is the basic means by which ritual is expressed in words. When worship becomes too intellectual or wordy, it loses its depth and significance. Our most fundamental understandings always begin in our intuitive, emotional world. It is only later, when we need to make sense out of our intuitive experiences, that the use of our intellects becomes significant. That should help us understand why children can be as meaningfully involved in ritual ceremonies as adults. But it should also help us understand why we should not permit our ceremonial life to become too intellectual. Of course, children can help prevent this. They can enable us to recapture a sense of spontaneity, mystery, and awe. They can help us understand and experience the power of real celebration.

I realized the significance of ritual for children on one occasion when I neglected a family ritual. For years, it was our family custom to celebrate the Sundays in Advent. During the ritual, the children would run about, talk, spill their milk, and appear to be totally disinterested and uninvolved. So one Sunday when I had to be away from home, my wife and I decided that our celebration could be delayed until my Monday evening return. However, upon my arrival home, I found two very upset children. I had neglected the family ritual. They missed it. It was more important to them than I had imagined.

It is in the realm of ritual that our main impasse lies today. It is at the level of symbolic action that our understandings begin. Before reflection, we must have experience. Ritual emerges from and brings into being the symbols by which life is made meaningful. The language of faith which conveys our perceptions is the language of symbolic actions. We kiss our children not only because we love them but so we can love them. We act our way into new ways of thinking, feeling, and willing. We make love so that we might fall in love. We make believe so that we might believe.

A person first learns Christ not as a theological principle but as an emotional confrontation that stimulates the imagination. A person learns first through action or experience, then through imagining or storytelling, and last through signs or theological concept-formation. Growth is a continual process. We express our faith in various ways at various times, but in point of fact we always know God symbolically. The experience of God belongs to all ages. Through our shared celebrations, we and our children come to know God. Why is it, then, that so many congregations discourage children from worshipping with them? Why is it that some people would keep children away from Holy Communion? Christ's real presence at the Eucharist is ultimately a mystery; it is a mystery that children not only can understand, but actually may understand better than adults.

The norm for understanding Christian life is expressed in the celebration of the Eucharist which can be described as a joyful gathering of God's storytelling people in which they proclaim their faith and share a common meal with their risen Lord. It is a celebration that unites all ages and provides us with a sense of community. Shared participation in celebrations of our faith refreshes and empowers both children and adults for ministry in the world. Children and adults belong together. Through a greater use of festivity, movement, and the arts they will receive the true benefit of ritual.

Together at our celebration we affirm the mystery and meaning of our lives. Together we experience a vision of the world as it is intended to be. Through our celebration we receive the power to transcend the boundaries of our everyday world of experience and reach out to those transcendent forces that refresh and renew us for our daily routine. Through celebration we find insight for tomorrow. When we share our celebrations with our children, our faith and lives are being shaped together.

That shouldn't be difficult for us to understand. We all love birthday parties and Thanksgiving family meals,

Fourth of July picnics, anniversary celebrations, and holiday festivities. Who among us does not like to dress up, decorate, parade, sing, dance, exchange gifts, and eat? Consider the celebration of baptism days, the Eucharist as a family meal, the Pentecost picnic, the anniversary day celebration of the saints, and holy day festivities. What are these celebrations without children? To accept children and thus to cater to our own childlike natures is to widen access for ourselves and our children to the world of God.

Some crucial questions we adults need to address are these: What occasions are we going to make special? How will we prepare? What will we do? What part of the story will we remember? What part of our story will we enact? How will we involve children? Only when ritual celebrations become central to the experience we share with our children will Christian faith come to life for us or for them.

PRAYING TOGETHER

Prayer is at the center of the Christian life. Prayer is communion with God, a personal response to God's presence. Prayer is conversation with God; it is listening and talking. Prayer is best understood when we compare it with a close friendship. We find that we like to be alone with a friend; it doesn't greatly matter what we are doing or, indeed, whether we are doing anything at all. Just to be in each other's presence is rewarding. If we are working on a project, collaboration is most satisfying when it is done with friends. We can discuss issues and ideas with anyone interested in them, but when we share with a friend, we share our feelings, our hopes and dreams, our failures and our hurts. With our friends, we not only talk and work, we just "waste time." We can sit or drive or walk, and nothing important needs to be accomplished beyond the fact that we are together in holy leisure. Signs of friendship are given through our bodies: we smile, wink, touch, embrace, kiss; to have a friend is to express our feelings in actions. Further, there are times when our friendship seems like a mountain-top experience and other times when it sinks to the deepest valleys. But most of life with our friends is lived in the plains. We don't demand of each other that we have peak experiences. We accept the fact that often our times together will be neither exciting nor traumatic. The life of prayer is like this relationship with a friend.

Whenever we face a crisis in faith, at its root is a crisis in prayer. To pray is to listen and to talk, but in prayer God first makes himself present to us. Prayer is our awareness and acknowledgement of God's presence. Prayer is what God does to us rather than anything we do to God. The beginning of prayer is to be aware of God's presence, to acknowledge it, and to express it: "Yes, God, you are with me; you do love me; you do want what is best for me." Prayer begins with a genuine opening to God.

The second step in prayer is to acknowledge our thanksgiving for God's presence. Gratitude is the obvious spontaneous outflow of being aware of God's presence and action in our lives. The third step is a loving response. It is to say to God "I love you too." And finally, we ask God, "What do you want me to know, to feel, or to do?" With that question expressed, we wait and listen for

God's response so that we might acknowledge that we have heard God and intend to change our life as God desires.

Of course, there are other ways to pray, but is it not strange that we often turn prayers solely into our own words—telling God what God already knows, neglecting to listen to God's response to our needs and desires? Prayer is really a way of life; it is our conscious relationship with God through adoration, confession, praise, thanksgiving, and intercession.

When we live in adoration, we focus on the heart and mind of God, asking nothing but to enjoy God's presence. Adoration is the life of the lover, the dreamer, and the visionary who views every aspect of life as a miracle. Confession is life lived under the judgement and grace of God. It is the life of those striving to bring their individual, interior experience and belief into harmony with their social, exterior practice and action. The life of praise is the life alive with the memory of the mighty acts of God. It is the life of dancing, singing, and praising God even in evil days. Thanksgiving is our celebrative awareness of God's continuing actions in our midst. It is the life that can still spy burning bushes, hear the voice of God, and grasp the presence of Christ in contemporary culture. Oblation is the offering of ourselves, our lives, and our labors for God's purposes. An intercession is the continuous striving to bring our wills in line with God's will, to live in continuous loyalty to the conviction that Jesus is Lord.

Last summer, I attended a conference in Evergreen, Colorado. One bright, cool, sunny day a small group of us packed some homemade bread, wine, and cheese and took off for the top of Mount Lewis. When we reached the top, we discovered a large patch of moss and wildflowers amid the snow. The scene left us strangely silent and uniquely aware of the presence of God; we began to make dance-like motions and sing in thanksgiving. Then we were silent again. Some children were with us. They were the first to pray.

It is unfortunate that so many people argue about whether or not children should be taught memorized prayers or simply how to speak with God spontaneously. We worry if children don't know their prayers, when the real issue is whether or not we ourselves are in a conscious relationship with God, a relationship that can take the form of talking or silence. Alone and together, that relationship may include either memorized ritual prayers that encourage the unconscious to experience the presence of God or spoken spontaneous prayers that bring the conscious mind into the presence of God.

The biggest issue we face in terms of prayer is our post-Reformation world-view. Our Judeo-Christian world-view affirms that God appears in healings, miracles, visions, dreams, and voices in the wilderness. Jesus taught that we can call upon the power that rules the universe. He taught that God speaks to us; he taught us a way of relating to God; he taught us the questions to bring before God. The Church called this prayer the "Lord's Prayer" or the "Our Father." The questions Jesus told us to ask were these:

Our Father in Heaven: What do you want to make possible in my life that neither I nor any other human being can make possible?

47

Holy is your name: What ordinary things in my life do you want to make holy?

Your kingdom come: How can your kingdom come through me?

Your will be done: What are my Gethsemanes, about which I need to say your will be done?

Give us today the bread we need: What nourishment or help do I need this day?

Forgive us our sins as we forgive those who sin against us: For what do I need to be forgiven and for what do I need to forgive others?

Save us from the evil one: What do I need to be protected from? To be a disciple is to listen for God's response to one's questions and to act accordingly.

But living the Lord's Prayer of course means accepting the concept of a spirit-filled world. For too long our world-view has been that human experience is bound by time and space; we have believed that knowledge comes only through sensual experiences and rational reflection; we have believed that miracles either never happened or happened once but no more.

There is, however, another world-view. Closer to modern science, which now supports the old Judeo-Christian position, this view says prayer is possible and reasonable. But in order to be part of that world-view, we will need to regain our God-given ability to wonder and create; to dream, imagine, and envision; to sing, to paint, to dance, to act. We will need to regain our natural capacity for ecstasy. We will need to regain the capacity for sensual and kinesthetic awareness; for appreciating the new, the marvelous, the mysterious; for being able to express ourselves emotionally and nonverbally. Of course we will not have to teach our children how to develop these capacities. They, on the other hand, can teach them to us. To share with our children a life in friendship with God is to pray and to learn to pray.

LISTENING AND TALKING TOGETHER

Children are always asking religious questions. We once asked the same questions; perhaps unconsciously we still do, but we put them aside or repress them. Children surface them for us, leaving us sometimes baffled or embarrassed. We need to acknowledge that many of their questions have no factual answers. But from the perspective of faith they all have answers.

Our responsibility is not to offer our children information, advice, or guidance. But children do deserve a response to their questions, an affirmation of their quest. We need to help them come into touch with the struggles, pains, doubts, and insecurities their questions reveal. The most profound questions of life have no answers; each only opens new questions that lead even deeper into the unspeakable mystery of and ultimately to the mystery of God. What our children are really asking is for us to reveal and share ourselves and our faith, not to provide dogmatic answers. We do not need to answer our children's questions, but we do need to make our faith available to them as a source for their learning and growth. We can offer our own experience, doubts and fears, questions, insights, and stories. We can say to them, "I don't know the answer, but I will help you search." "I just don't know how to explain it, but together we might discover some insight." You see, it is in the relationship between us during our shared quest that God is revealed.

First, however, we need to learn to listen—not just to the spoken question, but to the child who is speaking. Children can help us ask our own questions, and if we will let them, they can push us to new insights, helping us to hear God's voice in response to our quest.

The most important aspect of questioning is the dialogue it establishes between us and God. Reflecting back on the questions children have recently put to me, I share them and my answers, not because they tell you what to answer, but because they illustrate a testimony to faith.

Who is God? God is someone who knows you by your name. You are very special to God and God loves you.

Can I see God? No, not directly, the way you see me. God is so different from us. We can't see him with our eyes, but we know God is with us.

Then where is God? God is everywhere in every place there is life, joy, beauty, love, and peace.

Is science right or is the Bible right? They both are, for they ask different questions. Science asks how something happened and the Bible asks why.

Why didn't God heal my grandmother when I asked him to? When you pray for someone you love, you always should ask God to give that person what God thinks is best. God knows better than we do what your grandmother needs to be happy. We may not understand, but we can put all our trust in God.

Is God going to punish me because I was bad? God never punishes us. We punish ourselves when we do things that are wrong. God always wants to help us. God always wants to forgive us. God always loves us no matter what. *What is heaven?* I don't know, except I long for it very much. It will be the happiest and best surprise party we will ever attend. Jesus tells us it is like a great feast of thanksgiving that never ends and where there are no strangers. He also tells us we will be alive and happy as never before. That's why I don't fear dying.

Why does God let people die? We were all born to die, but people die for many different reasons. We all die someday, but when we do we are given a new life, and we will see God and have a party with God's friends.

On and on go the questions and their responses. In one sense none of my responses are answers to the question asked, but each is an attempt to share my faith in the mystery that is God. That is what it means to listen and talk together.

PERFORMING FAITHFUL ACTS OF SERVICE AND WITNESS

Faith is an active engagement in the service of God's Kingdom. Faith cannot exist without a commitment to the implementation of God's will. Faith first requires a way of perceiving, a vision of the Kingdom of God; it then requires a way of relating or living in the presence and companionship of God; and finally, it requires a way of acting with God in the world.

Faith is a creative act of the whole person, the power of God liberating and reconciling us to God and to each other. Faith involves more than mind, heart, or will; it is all three together. As such, faith is expressed and com-

51

municated through our style of life. Faith and good works always go together. You cannot have one without the other. To be Christian is to live under the merciful judgment and inspiration of the Gospel to the end that God's will is done and God's Kingdom comes.

Remember it was the life of Christians in the world that brought others to Christian faith. We are called to join in God's liberating and reconciling work in the world on behalf of peace, justice, and love. God is biased toward acts on behalf of those who are denied God's intentions. We are called to join in God's history-making; we are called to be a sign and witness to God's Kingdom come.

The Gospel of John reveals that Jesus learned through imitating God. The disciples were in turn to learn through imitating Jesus. We are to do likewise so that our children might imitate us. In the final analysis, then, we communicate our faith through our acts.

Jesus said, "As the Father sent me, so I send you" (John 20:21). Jesus asks us if we love him and then tells us what it means to love him; it means to feed his sheep, to care for and serve others, to be willing to die for our neighbor's good, and to restore people to unity with God and each other. The Christian faith implies a way of life. To share our faith is to share our life, to be an example, to give our children a glimpse of what the Christian life is. We need to share our lives of service, and we must invite our children to join us. That is what it means to live together with our children and share our faith.

CHAPTER FOUR

SHARING
THE ADOLESCENT
QUEST

IN THE United States we have created a unique youth culture of persons aged twelve to twenty-four; we call them adolescents. But I remember my first international youth gathering in Europe some twenty years ago. I took a group of fifteen-year-olds with me only to discover that most of the European youth were in their late twenties and early thirties. In Europe it appeared that people were considered children until they were sixteen, they were youth until they were thirty-five, and they were adults after thirty-five. The confusion expressed in the use of the term *adolescence* is an indication of the confusion that exists over the meaning of the word itself.

There was no defined adolescence before 1904. In that year the psychologist G. Stanley Hall wrote a book by that title and the term was born. Adolescence is now defined as a time of life between the end of childhood and the beginning of adulthood. The word itself comes from the Latin word *adolescere*, which means to grow up.

We describe adolescence as the time when people establish their identity, achieve a sense of autonomy and competence, learn self-control and the management of emotions, develop purpose and integrity, and achieve healthy interpersonal relations. But these are all aspects of a lifelong quest. We are always working at the establishment of our identity. This is not only a problem for adolescents, but the central question of the three-year-old who asks, Who am I? and the forty-year-old who asks, Am I satisfied with my life? As we read about the adolescent quest, we must never forget this fact. To some extent, all phases of faith and development intermingle throughout our lives. The need for ritual, storytelling, praying together, listening to and answering questions does not disappear at age twelve, or even at age fifteen. Adolescence simply represents a time in a person's life when certain aspects of human development express themselves in particular ways. Remembering that fact will help us relate to our children during their adolescence.

Nevertheless, the period from eleven or twelve to twenty-four or twenty-five years of age is a significant time. During that wide span of years people attain physical, sexual, and intellectual maturity. During the same years, they are apt to break from the moral and social norms of the community and experiment with alternative lifestyles; to have conflicts with parents and other authority figures; to drop out of church, church school, youth fellowship, and other nurturing institutions; to doubt and question the beliefs, attitudes, and values with which they were raised; to forsake earlier forms of religious piety; and to vacillate day to day from childish to mature behavior. So it is that the adolescent years are described as a difficult but satisfying time at best and as a period of stress and turmoil for youth and their parents at worst.

Every family lives through adolescence, but each experiences those years differently. Regretfully we have blown the adolescent years out of proportion, and in doing so, have turned them and our children into problems. By focusing on adolescence as an issue, we have treated certain human needs as though they belonged only to adolescence when, in reality, we address those same needs throughout our lives.

Perhaps adolescence is difficult for some of us middle-aged parents to cope with because we find ourselves struggling with the same issues our children are struggling with. Our youth, therefore, may highlight our own confusions, identity problems, doubts, struggles, lack of maturity, restlessness, discontent, and faithlessness. The best way to help our children work at life's issues during the years following childhood is to work at these issues ourselves from the vantage point of our age and experience. This may seem easier to contemplate if we remember that God has embraced them and us in his reconciling love. God has led us in the past and will continue to do so, through both the difficult and easy days together.

From the years of early adolescence and on, youth are beginning to search, question, judge critically, and experiment through the use of reason and argumentation rather than through feelings and experiences. Faith will often express itself in the form of doubt and the struggle to frame philosophical formulations. Through this personal search for truth, the adolescent moves from dependence on others' understandings and ways to a state of autonomy. To find a faith of their own, adolescents need to doubt, question, and test what has been handed down to them. They need to criticize the tradition in which they were brought up and to question their own feelings and experiences. During this period, we as parents need to be especially sensitive to the fact that changes don't necessarily mean that faith is being discarded; it may only be that the expressions of faith which belonged to others—often parents—now need to become uniquely those of the adolescent.

Adolescents need parents to support them in their quest, have confidence in them, and affirm them in their struggle with those beliefs, attitudes, and patterns of behavior in which they have been reared. Parents need to listen if they are to be an encouragement in the quest for a personal faith. Rather than try to *give* adolescents faith, parents should encourage them to do their own believing. Adolescents want acceptance, not approval; empathy and genuineness, not sympathy and pretense; they want affirmation of personhood, not approval of every act they perform.

It is important to provide our adolescents with freedom for their struggles of soul. In the Jewish bar or bat mitzvah ritual the parents pray: "Blessed be God who has taken away my responsibility for my child's conduct." We Christians need a similar rite of responsibility for adolescents. At such an occasion it would be appropriate for parents to pray: "Thank you God for taking away the responsibility we have borne for our children's faith and conduct." All parents, for their souls' sake, need to pray such a prayer, and all adolescents need to hear their parents pray it. Sometimes we have to celebrate our mutual liberation in order to unite in common efforts to grow in faith together.

In spite of their desire for freedom, however, adolescents also want limits in the forms of norms or guidelines. Actually, what they want and need most is the company of mature adults who are willing to share their struggles and intellectual quest for a truth they can live by for the rest of their lives. How this sharing is done will vary with each home situation. Again, the essential element is being available and interested when the questions come, in the same way one is available for a child. Sometimes the questions are unrecognizable because they are camouflaged in hostile feeling or argument. Then, if we are not alert and caring, we will miss the opportunity to play a supportive role.

The model for the parent of an adolescent is found in St. Luke's Emmaus road account. This is a story about a mysterious stranger who joins the disciples and walks along the road with them only a few days after Jesus' death. He asks only two questions and spends the rest of the time listening deeply to them as they tell of the Jesus of Nazareth who had disappointed them. As the disciples looked back on that experience, they confessed that it was the stranger's presence during the journey that was most memorable.

Of course, to be parents with such a presence we need to be mature in life and faith. If we are to be fellow pilgrims and guides on the journey, we need to have been there before. We also need to be working on our own faith and be willing to share our continuing journey with our youth. Only then can we speak openly and credibly of our own faith experience and share the truth of the Christian faith as it has been made known to us.

In evaluating our own faith, it is important to acknowledge that our human longings for religious meaning can express themselves in either negative or positive ways. These opposite forms have special meaning to parents of adolescents. In *Christian Believing*, Urban T. Holmes and I described them as "a religion of involvement" and "a religion of escape."

Religion can be a healthy response to life. When religion serves our human strengths, it is best understood as involving us in life's struggles, as being rational, and as being expressive of self-direction.

A religion of involvement is dedicated to the pursuit of meaning and value in human life. Aware that the world cannot meet our deepest needs, we find in religion an instrument for our progressive strivings after a sense of transcendent purpose for life. Just as important, it becomes a catalyst directing our lives toward a vision of a better life. It looks to the future and uses the past as leverage to move toward that future.

A religion of involvement is difficult; its demands are profound; it points the pilgrim to a risky path. It offers not safety but an opportunity to find new and unexpected maturity. Its adherents do not use the Church and its liturgy for escape and comfort, but for challenge and empowerment. Their concern is not to judge or convert people who believe differently, but to live faithfully with them. Believing that they themselves are accepted, their concerns are the world and the struggle for justice.

This type of religion meets head-on the challenge of the intellect. While it does not assert that one can know God by the power of one's mind, it certainly accepts reason and its cultivation as a gift of God. Beliefs are accepted only after they appear reasonable. These believers do not assume that there is conclusive proof of the existence of God. Nor do they seek something that "explains" it all. They are simply aware that the more they push back the horizons of their knowing, the more aware they are of the infinite *more* to be explored.

They, therefore, live with a childlike openness to the *more* that lies in life's mystery. They strive to perceive the subject that lies beyond their experience. For these open-minded people, reasons and emotion, intellect and intuition are all aspects of human life and essential for religious discovery. Still they seek to subject their religious convictions to a thorough intellectual analysis.

As might be expected, these people are self-directed. While they do not know all the answers and do not have an authoritarian source for their beliefs, attitudes, and actions, they consciously strive to act morally. They have internalized norms for life consistent with their beliefs, and principles to be used as they rationally attempt to mediate between their norms and the moral situations in which they find themselves.

Those with a "religion of involvement" have strong egos; they can face challenges, live in ambiguity and with change, and still maintain their equilibrium as they willingly move into the unknown as a necessary condition of growth. This does not mean that they are free from fear, but that they fear the slavery of the known more than the price of freedom.

A religion of escape, on the other hand, is defensive; it aims to protect one from alien forces. It offers harbor in a sea of storms. It comforts and promises peace of mind. Such a religion is functionally effective because it gives answers and leaves no questions. This also means that it is intolerant, moralistic, dogmatic, and rigid. Truth is known. One accepts it or rejects it; there is no continuing revelation. It is a religion of exclusion. It must by nature divide people into "we" and "they," at best considering the "they" as unenlightened and in error and at worst shunning and condemning them to hell. There is no room in this form of religion for the questioning of the adolescent. A religion of escape can be a pitfall for youth. In their search for a personal faith, adolescents may be sidetracked by the lure of security or comforting authoritarianism. Parents who sense that this is happening will accomplish little by admonishing their teenagers. Again, the parental role is to guide, encourage, share, even allow what we think to be a mistake—but always to provide love and care for the young person.

As we have pointed out, the adolescent is facing the same issues we all face throughout our lifetime, but in a particular way. Children and mature, healthy adults are always asking questions, but beginning at about age sixteen, people develop the ability to respond differently to the questions than they have been able to before. That is significant. During the adolescent years most people first acquire the ability to use their intellects. It is, therefore, essential that they do so. And this new capability needs to be applied to faith.

It is now reasonable to expect that adolescents will think objectively about themselves and the world of ideas; that they can understand that two statements which appear to negate each other can both be true depending on what questions you ask; and that they can envision a wide range of alternative solutions to a problem. As the concreteness and literalism of childhood disappears, adolescents understand the use of metaphors and allegories. And as they grow older they will be able to accept ambiguities and use analogies. Of course, these reasoning processes come slowly, and some adolescents begin later than others. For most adolescents, mature intellectual functioning involving abstractions, analysis, synthesis, and evaluation is yet to be developed. That is why decisions are very difficult for adolescents; that is also why important decisions, such as firm commitment to beliefs, should be avoided. In early adolescence youth have just begun to acquire the abilities necessary for an evaluation of the religious tradition they have received. They need to work at that task before they are called upon to make a decision of conviction. Decisions made during the early adolescent years will tend to be emotional rather than intellectual. These are times for wise listening and shared thinking on the part of the parent. Mature decisions should not be hurried. Instead, as adults we need to be *involved* in our own faith's intellectual quest so that we can encourage and support our adolescent children in the beginning of theirs.

In this regard, we need to admit that anti-intellectualism has always been present in our culture. Americans are not inclined to think of the gaining of knowledge as an end in and of itself. Although we spend millions of dollars on education, education is typically understood as having value because it is the way we reach another goal—in a job, for example. The intellectual quest for truth is not seriously valued. Those who pursue it are considered somewhat

strange if not impractical. Those who can produce practical, usable goods and services are usually paid more than
philosopher-theologians. Entertainers, comedians, popular
musicians, and athletes are considered of greater value
than the people who make up the humanities faculty of a
university.

Likewise, in the world of religion, groups with a
strong emphasis on feelings are inevitably more popular
than those faiths that affirm thought, or the religion of
the head. Indeed, among many such groups, to think
seriously about belief is considered dangerous. To be sure,
thoughtful questioning of beliefs has shaken the foundations of more than one person's life. Such intellectual
activity will continue to be "disturbing," but that ought
not to be considered unfortunate. In our own day, for
example, we cannot ignore the implications of the fact
that our Judeo-Christian tradition has been male-oriented.
We need to question the assumptions that value such beliefs. But if God can no longer be thought of only as
"father" or referred to only as "he," what is to become of
the beliefs of our ancestors? That question ought not to
frighten us.

While irrational faith has always been condemned by
the Church, the denial of reason and the equation of
sentiment and truth appear always to have plagued the
Christian community. It is at this point that thoughtful
parents can help thoughtful adolescents understand that
believing is a basic function of human reason and imagination and that beliefs should be arrived at as a result of
logical, rational reflection on experience. If searching
youth are not given guidance here, they may be among

those who, turned off by irresponsible forms of pietism, leave the Church.

An intellectual love of God is reverence in the face of mystery, a trustful curiosity, a restless searching and doubting, an affirmation of the spirit of wonder sustained by the tacit confidence that there is an order of truth beyond and within the manifold puzzle of the present order. Doubt is not a foe, but the friend of understanding. Doubt keeps faith relevant and dynamic; an intellectual love of God keeps reason from cynicism and skepticism.

The authority of the Church is like a three-legged stool, the legs being the Scriptures and Church tradition, our experience in community, and reason. Remove one leg and the stool topples over.

The Bible contains a unique testimony of God's self-disclosure. It contains the record of God's Word, God's past actions and future intentions. But the Bible is a human product, a result of the Church's experience and history. We need to learn how to read it and comprehend it. It is not enough just to know the stories as we did in childhood; we need to learn what its human writers wanted their audiences to understand. Only then can we be faithful in our attempts to understand what the Bible says to us and apply those truths to our lives.

In the adolescent quest, parents and youth can experiment with studying the Bible together. In an open, informal setting, this can be an exciting, rewarding experience. In the process of working at interpretations, both youth and adults can use intellects and all the tools of scholarship to look critically at the biblical text in its historic setting and thus interpret it accurately and faithfully.

We cannot live faithfully unless we are willing to study the Scriptures of the Old and New Testaments seriously and critically and then to meditate on their word for us.

We also must remember that Christianity is founded on a historical perspective. We have to know both our history and our traditions if we are to have a mature faith.

We need to offer our youth an example of the use of faith and reason in our own moral actions. Each day we must make decisions and accept the consequences of our action or inaction. Each day, then, we confront the question of life's meaning and the world's purpose. Even small actions are indicative of fundamental values. And when the demand of situation and the norms of faith seem to conflict, we need to know how to use intelligently the Christian principle of liberating and reconciling love.

The words of Jesus are a call to sincere and resolute deeds of just love toward all peoples. If we do not act accordingly we have no right to the name *disciple*. "Why do you keep calling me 'Lord'—and never do what I tell you?" (Luke 6:46)

James wrote, "Here is one who claims to have faith and another who points to his deeds. To which I reply, 'Prove to me that this faith you speak of is real though not accompanied by deeds, and by my deeds I will prove to you my faith.'" (James 2:18)

If thoughtful adolescents have left the Church because of disillusionment over anti-intellectual responses to the Christian faith, a great number have also become cynical over the lack of response to need in the world. Part of the adolescent quest leads to struggles with the problems of personal responsibility in this area.

Instead of assuming responsibility, we adults sometimes accuse God of not working in the world. But it is not God who is absent; we are absent. Instead of wondering why God allows people to starve, we need to examine with our adolescents why we allow people to hunger and thirst. The gift of reconciling love in the Spirit has set us free to live and work for others.

When we speak of a "personal relationship with Jesus Christ," we are speaking of a calling to witness for justice, peace, equality, liberation, community, and the well-being of all peoples. Our relationship with Christ demands that we never fall victim to life as it is.

It matters what we believe. It matters how we believe. It matters what values we hold. It matters what vision has captured our imaginations. It matters why we live and for what we live. To live our own lives faithfully day by day in the world is the best and most important gift we can give our adolescents to aid them in their struggles with the Christian faith.

CHAPTER FIVE

MODELING THE ADULT PILGRIMAGE

WE have children when we seem least emotionally and intellectually prepared to raise them. It is a time in our lives when we ourselves have so many needs that it is difficult to meet theirs. By the time our children have reached adolescence, we have entered middle age. We may joke about life beginning at forty, but we secretly fear it will end there. Middle age seems to activate our deepest anxieties. Engulfed by new strains and tensions, we have difficulty responding to the stress and turmoil of our youth.

What, pray tell, is an adult? One thing is certain: an adult is not a person who has arrived. Like childhood and adolescence, adulthood is both a chronological fact and a psycho-social expression of one point in our human pilgrimage to fulfillment.

A mass of literature has been produced on childhood and adolescence. These terms are identified as the formative growth periods in our life. Then somehow, when we are less than halfway through our life span, we automatically become adults and are no longer in need of growth or development. As adults, we are responsible for sharing the lives of others and aiding our children's growth. I suggest that it is just this mind-set that makes it difficult for parents to help their children in their pilgrimage. Growth is a never-ending, lifelong process. The status of adulthood and maturity are not the same. To be a healthy adult is to be growing and developing. Indeed, some of our most significant growth is possible only during the adult years.

If some children never seem to mature and some youth never seem to leave adolescence, it may be because the adults in their lives also stopped growing and so were unable to provide them with role models for growth and maturity. If we really love our children, if we really want them to grow in Christian faith, we need to spend more time working at our own growth in faith.

Of course, it is difficult during our adult years to find the time to address the religious aspect of our lives. During early adulthood we face tremendous demands as we seek to find our place in the world of work, to marry and begin a family, to assume heavy financial commitments, and to become independent people. No sooner have we dealt with these demands than, between the ages of thirty and forty, another traumatic transition confronts us. Now we face the crisis of modifying or giving up earlier dreams and re-evaluating the implication of past decisions on the next stage in our lives. During all these years the pressures of parenthood are ever present. The demands of work and home, community and church on our time and energy frustrate us. We discover that having children does not necessarily improve a marriage; as a matter of fact, children may strain the relationship. We learn that child-rearing is not fun; it may be meaningful and rewarding but never pure pleasure. We become aware that love may be a necessary ingredient in a marriage, but it is never enough.

If I have learned anything over the years, it is this: We need to make the religious aspects of our lives a priority; we need to make our growth in faith our first commitment in terms of time and energy. Only then can we deal with our own anxiety, admit that we will never be the perfect parent, and acknowledge that our children are in God's hands. Then we can relax, and instead of trying to live for our children, we can live for ourselves and share ourselves with them. Only when we turn to our own faith and life do we have anything to share with our children. That is what this chapter is about; it is an invitation to work out our salvation, to continue the journey begun at our baptism, to engage ourselves seriously in the pilgrimage of faith so we might live faithfully with our children and thereby bring them up in the Christian faith.

When we were young, we needed to be introduced to and nurtured in the Christian faith and life. When we reached adolescence, we needed to be encouraged to deal critically and intellectually with the faith into which we had been nurtured. Now during our adult years, we need to direct our attention strongly toward our further maturation in the Christian faith and life.

Mature faith comes about by a uniting of the faith of our childhood with the probing of adolescence and young adulthood. When we reach this point, we are governed neither by the authority of the community nor by our own authority, but by a union of God and self. We are secure enough in our convictions now to challenge the community when conscience dictates, but we no longer need always to be critical or negative. Doubt, of course, never ends, but those with mature faith have a clear sense of their identity and are open to new experiences which aid them in a process of continuing growth and development. They have closer relationships to God and act more consistently with God in the world. Persons of mature faith acknowledge both their responsive-intuitive-affective nature and their active-intellectual-rational nature. They move easily back and forth from experience to reflection and the need to make sense of their experience.

To be Christian is to be always moving toward the completeness of our humanity, which in one sense we always possess as a gift from God and which in another sense we never reach except in eternity.

For most people, *vocation* means merely *career*, but to the Christian, vocation is first and foremost our response to God's call to fulfillment. There are times when we ask, Do our lives lead anywhere? Are we going someplace? Our Christian faith explains that the goal of human life is nothing less than life with God. And the good news is that we are destined for and able to share in the life of God.

The Old Testament contains dramatic descriptions of the ways in which our ancestors lived their vocations. With Abraham, a new chapter in salvation history began. It was previously unheard of that a person should at the "call" of God leave home and kin, tear up roots, and become a pilgrim. Thus, a new meaning was given to "faith," and Abraham and Sarah became prototypes for *vocation*. Faith ever after has been a response to a call from God, a covenant relationship between God and God's people to share in a journey toward fulfillment. Human life is a journey home!

Whom we love makes a difference in this journey. St. Augustine put it this way: "Good or bad loves make good or bad lives." The kind of person with whom we fall in love makes all the difference in the shape, quality, and direction of our lives. If we are so deeply affected by our worldly loves, how much more are we affected by our love relationship with God? To "come home" is to have an intimate relationship with God; indeed, the deepest longing of the human heart is to be "at home" with God. At least that is the way many of the saints have interpreted the deep stirrings within themselves. The psalmist expressed it beautifully when he wrote:

> As a hind longs for the running streams,
>   so do I long for thee, O God.

> With my whole being I thirst for God, the living
>   God.
> When shall I come to God and appear in his
>   presence?

> (Psalms 42:1-2)

The Bible is a love story, the record of a people living in a love relationship with God. It is also the record of our human failure to love God faithfully.

For Christians to love God is to be God's faithful people, to live under the rule of God, to do God's will, and to live in a relationship with God, our neighbor, ourselves, and the natural world.

Our calling, now as in the past, is to transform our work, profession, or trade into a context and means for witnessing to the coming of God's Kingdom. At its deepest level, Christian life is a call to service, or ministry, and to mission, or witness. Since we all do not bring the same gifts or have opportunities for the same influence, our personal ministries take different shapes and forms. But none is superior to any other. None is more holy. Our common vocation is fulfilled when each faithfully performs her or his unique personal ministry and supports others in theirs.

When our daily lives are understood as ordained by God, everything we do is transformed; God is served and glorified by our lives. God says, "Act as a believer in Jesus Christ and a member of his Church where you are and as you are!" And God further, through the Holy Spirit, makes possible the means by which we can do so.

Jesus clearly demonstrates vocation fulfilled. He established the reign of God; he brought God's Kingdom into being. After Pentecost, to the astonishment of everyone, the remarkable spiritual power that had been witnessed in Jesus was seen in his followers. The Apostles acknowledged their call to citizenship in God's Kingdom and they were empowered to witness to its coming.

The Kingdom of God is the power of God expressed in actions directed toward a new social order in which the well-being of all is fulfilled and equality, liberation, and justice are manifest. The time is now, said Jesus; the reign of God is here; change your life and commit yourself to live for and in the good news that a new possibility for individual and social life is now present. The vocation of the Christian is to proclaim in word and deed the Gospel of God's Kingdom coming.

Peter writes: "But you are a chosen race, a royal priesthood, a dedicated nation, and a people claimed by God for his own, to proclaim the triumphs of him who has called you out of darkness into his marvellous light" (1 Peter 2:9). Restated, Peter reminds us: You have been blessed and called to the awesome, undeserved responsibility of living so close to God that you might represent God before all peoples. Through both your deeds and words you are called to witness to the gracious acts of God which transform lives and all of life.

For some, the Christian life has been understood as a private, otherworldly, anti-intellectual, emotional affair. This is a misinterpretation of the Gospel. Authentic Christian piety is both individual and corporate, "otherworldly" and "this-worldly," intellectual and emotional, contemplative and active.

You and I are spiritual beings for whom God intends integrated lives of both love of God and love of neighbor. As such, our life is neither exclusively practices (such as acts of worship) nor good works (such as acts of charity), nor is it solely an interior life blind to external social and political realities.

When we live in the Spirit we become vehicles for God's transformation, the medium through which God is remaking the human world. Within this world, where the majority of people live in estrangement, poverty, hunger, and injustice, we Christians bear the social imperative of being faithful to the mission of our Lord. Christ brought good news to the poor and sick, called the well to act

75

and the healthy to repentance, proclaimed in deed and word release to the captives, restored sight to the blind, liberated the oppressed, and announced the arrival of God's rule of liberating and reconciling love. His words *and* his deeds witnessed to God's coming community.

To live in the Spirit is to be a bearer of this Gospel tradition. Our vocation is to live consciously in the presence of God, who acts through persons and communities; it is to live in a conscious awareness of God's redeeming and empowering presence, just as it is also to live in the political and social arena on behalf of justice and peace.

Life in the Spirit is a gradual and deliberate harmonization of our lives in relationship to the natural world, to others, to ourselves, and to God. This kind of life can be compared to playing in a symphony orchestra. We are all players who, while related to one another, do not all play the same notes. Some, for a while, carry the melody while others stick to those ongoing bass rhythms which provide a foundation for the melody. In some moments, some of us do not play at all; we wait until it is our turn once again.

At times in our lives, some of us will express a dominant concern for social and political priorities. Others will concentrate on relationships nearer home. From time to time we need to take stock of ourselves, of who and where we are in our pilgrimage. At various times we are all called to the quiet and open contemplation of God. It is all of us together that make the music, and the symphony requires each one of us to play with all our heart the part that has been given to us.

The trouble is that so many of us assume that we should all be playing exactly the same part at the same time: this is not so. People passionately concerned with social justice, parents struggling to bring up a family, people discovering themselves through psychoanalysis, and those involved in a life of contemplative prayer are all part of one great symphony. Insofar as each one of us is committed to Christ, each of us is in harmony with the others, and each of us needs to affirm the others' part. Each one of us needs to learn to listen intently to the tunes others are playing and to the deeper rhythms that bind us all together.

Sometimes we overemphasize our relationship to the world and to others at the expense of our relationship to God and to the inner self. When this happens, worldly and social concerns become shallow, empty, and foundationless and soon lose their vitality. However, when the relationships to God and our innermost selves are overemphasized, to the exclusion of the political, social world, they can easily become selfish, self-absorbing, and sinful. At different times, some within the Body of Christ may need to emphasize a particular aspect of the whole. Some will need to focus on their primary relationship to God. Others will need to focus on the healing of their inner wounds, while still others will need to focus on caring for the neighbor in distress. Each member needs the support and affirmation of the others. Those with a mystical turn of mind need fellow Christians to encourage them to look at the practical world and its wants. Others need to hear what the mystic has discovered about the relationship with human life.

What I cherish for myself and each of you is a vision of who, by God's grace, we are and therefore are called to become.

On our pilgrimage, to actualize our true self, we need to make time for these particular endeavors:

Times to struggle with ourselves. The biblical story of Jacob wrestling with God reveals our necessary struggle with the dark and unknown parts of ourselves—the hurts, fears, and unanswered questions of who and whose we are.

Times to be with others in community. We need times to share longings and hopes, our cares and sorrows, our trials and tribulations, our joys and accomplishments, our happiness and fulfillment.

Times to reflect on our gifts and talents, our possibilities and challenges, our calls to service.

Times to have dialogues with God, to be still and listen, to speak and shout, to be in relationship with and without words with what is within and without us.

Times to connect with the world around us, to see and hear afresh, to open ourselves to new experiences, understandings, and ways of life.

Times to record what is happening to us and to reflect on our lives, to gain new insights into and awareness of life.

Times to dream and be grasped by visions.

Times to seek help from companions along the way, to permit others to aid our growth, to relate to one another and to God.

Times to pray alone and to worship with others, to acquire the strength which fits us for service.

Times to grow in wisdom; to engage in the search for goodness, truth, and beauty; to be self-critical and alert to the lessons of experience, especially the anomalies and contradictions that experience reveals; to learn and grow from our experience in the light of our tradition.

Times to acknowledge our bodies and their needs for exercise and rest, for eating and fasting, for singing and dancing, for making love and sleeping.

Times to relate to nature, to look at a rock, to hear water flow in a stream, to see the sun rise and set, to plant, to smell a flower, to pet a dog.

Times to serve, to help another in need, to care, to be with another person, to listen, to hug, to feed the hungry, to free the captive, to clothe the naked, to bring a cup of water to the thirsty.

Times to play.

Times to work, physically and mentally, to do both simple work and hard labor.

Times to study, to read and reflect, to allow for struggles of the mind.

Times to act, to engage in politics and economic and social change.

Times to develop political skills and know-how in institutional reforms.

Times to read the Bible alone and with others.

Times to worship in celebration and penitence, alone and in community.

Times to enhance our intuitions and passions, to feel and express our emotions.

Times to retreat for meditation and contemplation, for silence and directed guidance and counsel.

Faith is a gift. By it we know that we are justified through grace, not by works. Still, we need a self-imposed discipline in the busy tempo of our lives that we might grow in grace. We need to establish times for the nourishment of our spiritual life: moments for a daily meeting with God, moments to reflect on these meetings, and moments committed to witnessing to the God we have met.

We need, also, to become more available to others in the world, so that their needs, joys, and hopes can become ours. Christian solitude is not, therefore, an escape from ourselves, other people, or from the world, its problems and its miseries. Christian service is a spontaneous and natural overflow from our solitude with God.

Christian presence in the world requires the ability to pay close attention to every aspect of life. Only when we listen can we properly respond to what God is calling us to do. When we have the courage to listen and the insight to respond, then things begin to happen. We discover, for example, that we can be agents of transfiguration far beyond our limited capacities and vision.

We all can recall those times when we have been totally and imaginatively present to another person. Being present in this way requires that we pay close attention to others as mysteries created by God. This loving presence to our brothers and sisters, to the whole of Creation, is required of every Christian. It is a sharing in the compassionate and loving gaze with which God regards the world. To live with and in God's world, with God's people, and with oneself involves compassion—the ability to enter imaginatively into the lives of others and to feel joy and pain with them.

If our brothers or sisters fail, then so have we. If they are touched with glory, given to visions, capable of heroism, then so are we. When we are truly present to one another we begin to see that there is one race, one destiny, that there is solidarity in sin and solidarity in glory! We belong to one another. We are what our brothers and sisters are, because as we have seen, we are made of the same stuff and stamped with the same image and likeness.

To serve in this way, we have to give up our desire to be either inferior or superior to others. We have to embrace an alarming doctrine of equality. But this is not the meaningless equality of a cooky mold. We are not all the same in that sense; we are not pressed out on a production line. There is, however, an equality of presence, an equality of life, an equality of our being children of the one Parent. Each one of us is bathed in an equal light. When we begin to understand that kind of equality, then the glorious differences between persons begin to emerge. There is, indeed, one human race—but what variety, what colors, what gifts!

In being present to God and to one another, we can enter into another person's pain or joy at that place where it can be shared. It is an exhilarating and fearful experience. This is not the easy camaraderie of persons loosened a little from their inhibitions by a couple of beers or a dry martini. It is the creative presence of a person who is content to wait and quietly enter the pain and the joy of another. There, we share the strange intimacy of our condition. We know that we are mortal. We know that we share a common destiny. It is there that we can begin to minister to one another. It is there, in the face of our death, that we are truly one, truly together, truly made of the same stuff.

While there is nothing we can do to earn salvation and we all know that love, joy, peace, patience, kindness, goodness, faithfulness, gentleness, and self-control are best understood as "the harvest of the Spirit" (Galatians 5:22), we need to practice these qualities. In a sense, unless we practice them, they are not ours, and in a sense, it is through practice that they become fully ours, that is, expressions of living in the spirit. Of course, we cannot do so alone, we need the Church, the community of faith.

Baptism is never a private act of a family. It is a public act of the Church. At this ceremony we reaffirmed our baptismal covenant with God and the Church, and the community doing likewise also welcomed our child into its family and promised before God to assume responsibility of our child's journey in the faith. So it is that from the start we are bound together. Our children need the Church; the Church needs them. The Church needs us and we need the Church. If we as parents are to fulfill our vows to share our faith with our children and to journey with them toward maturity, we will need the aid of others in the community of faith. The challenge before us all is to so live together in the Church that the journeying begun at our baptism may be faithful to our calling.

As I complete this book, I am humbled by the sense of expectancy I have experienced throughout the Church for spiritual guidance. I am aware of the changing movements in the universe: here and there the dark, inward time of winter stillness, seemingly without life, and here and there the color and warmth of spring and the bursting forth of new life. We each pass through all these seasons during the course of our own life as well. It is awesome to see a new generation discovering their true humanity and the spiritual source of all life. Hopefully, we will be granted the grace to move gracefully with the awareness and changes confronting us, incorporating in our spiritual lives solitude and community, contemplation and action.

The human heart constantly seeks new insight into the meaning of life in order to live it more fully, joyfully, enthusiastically. At the root of this search for life and meaning is a search for God, the creator of life and author of its meaning. There never seems to be enough time for the search. Still we struggle on. My prayer is that this book may contribute to our journey together in the quest for life lived in the Spirit of God.

HISTORICAL REFLECTIONS ON PARENTS' ROLE IN CHRISTIAN NURTURE

IN THE early Church, the Christian nurture of children was the parents' fundamental duty, a duty which could not be delegated. As early as the fourth century St. John Chrysostom wrote a treatise entitled *On the Right Way for Parents to Bring up Their Children*. From the first to the fifteenth centuries pronouncements were issued condemning parents for the neglect of their children's nurture and cajoling them to assume their God-given responsibility. It was only because parents often neglected their obligation that other means were instituted. Still the conviction remained that the training children received in the home from their parents was the most important of all.

Erasmus in the fifteenth century stressed the central importance of home life, parental example, and direct parental religious and moral instruction of children. The home, he believed, was responsible for laying the foundation of all Christian education. Sir Thomas Elyot, in the first book on education written in English, in the sixteenth century, emphasized the significance of the early years and wrote that from the day children are born they will be blessed or cursed by their parents' example and home environment. Martin Luther emphasized the role parents play in the education of the children and urged fathers to instruct their children in religion at least once a week. He wrote: "[Parents] should know that they can perform no better and no more useful work for God, Christianity, the world, themselves and their children than by bringing up their children well. . . . Nothing is of value in comparison with the right training of children, for that is the straight road to heaven. . . ." Luther went on to suggest that people who could not instruct their children in religion should not be married. He wrote, "No one should become a father unless he is able to instruct his children . . . so that he may bring up true Christians." For Luther religious education was the first duty of parenthood.

John Calvin frequently preached on parents' responsibility for the religious education of their children. It was only through parents, explained Calvin, that children were included in the covenant and thereby qualified for baptism. It was, therefore, the duty of pastors to supervise the daily conduct of parents and the nurture of their children.

In the seventeenth century, John Comenius held that the Christian home was the primary agency for molding a child's religious nature.

The responsibility of parents for the nurture of their children was taken seriously by the Puritans of both England and New England. In 1642 Massachusetts enacted a law requiring parents to catechize their children in the principles of religion at least once each week. They taught that if parents who had received the covenant of grace did not help their children receive it also, they would fail to fulfill the terms of the covenant and might lose its benefits themselves. In his *Farewell Exhortation*, Richard

Mathew imagined children whose education had been neglected addressing their parents at the day of judgement with these words: "All this that we here suffer is through you. You should have taught us the things of God and did not. . . . You were the means of our original corruption and guiltiness and yet you never showed any care that we might be delivered from it . . . woe unto you that you had no more compassion and pity to prevent the everlasting misery of your own children."

For Rousseau, in the eighteenth century, the nurture of children began at birth in the home. He insisted that there is no vice or goodness in a child that is not caused by parents. For Pestalozzi, the home and family were the key to Christian nurture. He wrote, "Where love is found in the home, children will know God."

Horace Bushnell, one of the most important voices in the history of Christian education in the nineteenth century, continued to emphasize the crucial role of the family in child nurture. In his seminal work *Christian Nurture*, Bushnell stressed his opinion that the family as a social group is such that the spirit and character of parents inevitably influences the lives and character of their children. Bushnell emphasized the quality of the parents' faith for the faith of their children. "Let every Christian father and mother," he wrote, "understand that when their child is three years old that they have done more than half of all they will ever do for their character." "Inevitably," he continued, "children absorb both the good and bad faults of their parents. It is through our parental example that our children's faith is determined." According to Bushnell, the fulfillment of true parenthood is impossible unless the parents are themselves Christians: "Have it first in yourselves, then teach it as you live it; teach it by living it for you can do it in no other manner."

George Albert Coe held similar convictions in the twentieth century. If God is to become a living power in the consciousness and conduct of children, he wrote, parents must habitually speak of God as an actual present reality in their own lives. For Lewis J. Sherill, the family was the first and most important school of the child. Parents, by what they themselves are and do, he said, furnish the material which makes up the child's idea of God.

In 1929 Pope Pius XI's encyclical *Divini Illius Magistri* strongly stated the family's responsibility for the religious education of their children. To support his position he quoted from St. Thomas, "Parents are under grave obligation to see to the religious and moral education of their children." In Vatican II *Declaration on Christian Education*, the responsibility of parents is affirmed once again. It reads: "Parents must acknowledge that they are the first and foremost educators of their children. Their role is so decisive that scarcely anything can compensate for their failure in it." In the *General Catechetical Directory* of 1971 we read, "In the families of believers the first months and years of life, which are of the greatest importance for a man's life in the years to come, already provide the right conditions for developing a Christian personality."

The responsibility of parenthood can turn our joy into despair. The pressures of family life and the burdens of parenthood press upon us in our day. Only when we acknowledge the Church as our family can we survive. Neither the single-parent family nor the nuclear family can bear alone the responsibility of Christian nurture. We need an extended family, the Church, to help us be faithful with our children and to support us in the nurturing of our children in Christian faith. Together with the aid of God's grace and the comfort of the Holy Spirit the future is hopeful.